10 Incredible Mistakes At GETTYSBURG

A review of the battle and how blunders
by the Generals shaped the outcome.

BY
HARRIS MULLEN

HIGH WATER PRESS
Tampa, FL

ISBN 0-9646629-0-6
Printed in the United States of America
Second Printing

10 Incredible Mistakes At
GETTYSBURG

HIGH WATER PRESS / 315 S. Arrawana Ave. / Tampa, FL 33609

Introduction:

Incredible

How could such mistakes have been made by the generals of both armies?

This writing examines ten incredible errors and the generals who committed them before, during, and after the three day battle.

It starts with Lee crossing the Potomac June 24, 1863 into Pennsylvania and ends with Lee recrossing the Potomac July 13, 1863 with Gen. Meade nipping (not very hard) at his heels.

The Battle of Gettysburg started with big mistakes which increased in scale as the three days passed. On the Confederate side the mistakes were mainly failure to use sound military tactics and poor communication which caused destruction and lost opportunities. Union failures were mostly the result of a lack of discipline. Collectively these mistakes shaped the direction of the battle and ultimately the outcome.

In examining why such mistakes were made at Gettysburg, we need to understand the attitude and motivation of the individual soldier. Reading letters from those who participated clearly reveals that most soldiers believed that this was "The big one." These men pushed themselves beyond human capacity in the name of saving their homes and country. Heroism was not new to many of them, but never before had so much valor and patriotism revealed itself in such large measure over three days of fighting.

Emotion and anxiety have always interfered with sound judgment and we have to believe that most of those who made the mistakes made them hoping to further their cause.

The erring generals are reviewed chronologically according to their performances during the battle.

Three Deadly Days (July 1 - 3, 1863)

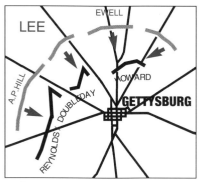

July 1 Hill's Confederate divisions moving toward Gettysburg on Chambersburg Pike run into stubborn resistance from Union cavalry in early morning. Fighting intensifies as both armies bring troops on the field. Finally Hill's and Ewell's Corps converge on Union forces from two directions and drive the Reynolds' (Doubleday) and Howard's Corps through the town of Gettysburg. Confederates win the day. Yankees fall back to Cemetery Hill and Ridge. Ewell decides that it is not "practicable" to attack Culp and Cemetery Hills. More Union corps arrive.

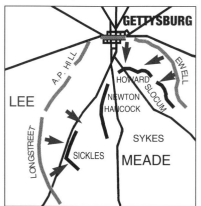

July 2 Both armies are on the battlefield or nearby. Lee, probing for a weak point in the Union line orders a coordinated attack on both ends of the Union line. Union III Corps (Sickles) moves off Cemetery Ridge exposing the entire Army but is saved by fellow officers. Fierce fighting occurs in The Peach Orchard, The Wheatfield, Devil's Den, and Little Round Top. Late in the day Ewell storms Culp's Hill but is pushed off the next morning. Day ends with heavy casualties on both sides with Union well entrenched.

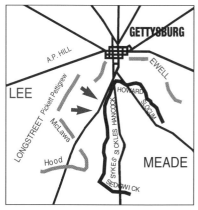

July 3 Lee believes the Union center is weak because of the disposition of Union troops. He orders an artillery assault by 140 cannons on the middle of Cemetery Ridge. Longstreet is slow getting into position. Ewell has been ineffective at Culp's Hill. After two hours of artillery fire directed at the Union center, Confederate divisions of Pickett, Heth (Pettigrew), and Pender (Trimble) lead the fatal charge over nearly a mile of open land. Lee is unable to break the Union line and on July 4 begins to withdraw. Gen. Meade allows the Rebel army to return to Virginia unchallenged.

10 Incredible Mistakes at Gettysburg

A review of the battle and how blunders by the Generals shaped the outcome

July 1, 1863 - July 3, 1863

The generals who participated in the Battle of Gettysburg were mostly U. S. Military Academy graduates. At West Point the dangers and consequences of making a tactical mistake on the battlefield were ingrained.

Ironically, the Confederate battle leader, Gen. Robert E. Lee, had taught military tactics to many on both sides of that field, and those he had not instructed in the classroom at the Military Academy, he had taught forcefully on a dozen battlefields during the past year.

Did Lee forget some of the textbook fundamentals he had taught?

Who made the mistakes at Gettysburg, and how badly did they hurt?

Mistakes, in fact, were starting to develop by the time Lee and his Army of Northern Virginia crossed the Potomac River into Pennsylvania. But neither Lee nor his jubilant fighting men seemed concerned.

By this time Lee's reputation had become legendary in the Confederacy. He was the symbol of victory. He could not be defeated. He and his army were invincible! His men were willing to "follow him to Hell!" as they put it.

This unbridled adoration of Confederate soldiers for their leader has intrigued writers and historians for generations. There is no doubt the recent, stunning victories at Fredericksburg and Chancellorsville, still fresh in their thoughts, swelled their sense of superiority. Lee's already brilliant reputation had skyrocketed. And it was in this aura that his men freely bathed themselves. Some 70,000 men, three corps, trudged northward with grim determination.

It is difficult now, however, to understand how Lee managed to maintain his confidence and state of well being and pass it along to his troops in view of the real status and condition of the Confederacy at that time. The war was going badly in the West and Grant had Vicksburg against the wall. Lee's army was severely under-supplied in both food and clothing, and was moving farther from its base of supply. Gen. "Stonewall" Jackson lay dead from wounds at Chancellorsville, two out of three of Lee's corps commanders were new and untried, and there was a serious short supply of field rank officers. Desertions were rampant and the hope of British recognition seemed slim or non-existent. And Lee's health at that time was none too good.

But while Lee kept his usual confidence alive, he was well aware of the dire situation. He had convinced Jefferson Davis and his Cabinet that the Confederacy's best option was to strike the enemy hard on its home turf. In fact it might have been the only real possibility of modifying the course of the war. The North's war machine and troop count was now going forward in full swing. The Confederacy's ability to recruit manpower in quantity and quality had started downhill months ago.

But Lee had whipped the Bluecoats before when the odds were not on his side. If he could win this one maybe he could change the North's mind about continuing the war. The Union was sick of the fighting. Abe Lincoln had been through a string of bumbling generals who had completely frustrated him and the populace. Union casualties were beginning to be viewed as willful slaughter. Violent draft riots were taking place, and the North was suffering from a bad military inferiority complex. Another serious Union defeat would surely be a disaster.

But Lee wanted more than just a defeat. He wanted to destroy the Army of the Potomac as a fighting unit, and he believed his beloved fighters were capable of it. So did they. With such a victory he could move on to capture Baltimore or Washington or both. This would cause the Union total despair.

Obviously, it would require a victory of huge proportions.

Lee, with his overwhelming influence had sold the plan over the objections of his fellow generals. Longstreet, Beauregard and Johnston, had made good cases for redirecting the South's dwindling military resources away from war-torn Virginia. Both Gens. Bragg in Tennessee, and Pemberton, besieged at Vicksburg, were begging for men and supplies.

The difficulties and the odds against success of the plan were extinguished by Lee's amazing record of longshot wins. Lee knew the South could not conquer the Union by driving its soldiers from the field. Its best hope was to continue to cause the North so terrible a loss of life and money that its citizens would rebel and negotiate a peace. The overriding question was whether the South could hold on that long.

Lee, better known for his tactical expertise than grand strategy had, in the end, chosen the course of greatest strategic potential for a dying army. If it was not timely strategy, it was certainly recognition of the facts. Lee knew the stakes were very high and the effort very risky. It was a move compatible with his offensive nature. The dramatic Northern thrust was the sort of warfare Lee liked best. Only Lee possessed the audacity to match the plan.

When Lee made his move northward it was obvious he did not expect Union Army commander Gen. Joe Hooker to follow him as quickly as he did. Lee's first target in Pennsylvania, in what would amount to a terror raid, was Harrisburg and he sent newly-minted Second Corps Commander Lt. Gen. Richard Ewell ahead of his other two corps to seize the prize. Ewell, who had lost a leg in battle under Jackson was often called "Old Bald Head," perhaps because of his advanced age of 46. Ewell had been a fine division commander but he was unproven as a corps leader.

Meanwhile, about a week before fighting started at Gettysburg, Lee ordered the flamboyant, but highly capable cavalryman, Maj. Gen. J. E. B. Stuart to attack Union supply lines and keep Hooker off balance should he follow Lee's move. He also ordered Stuart to guard Ewell's right flank as his corps moved northward and keep him (Lee) posted on the movements of the Army of the Potomac.

As Lee moved northward Stuart was strangely silent and for a time Lee assumed that Hooker had not yet crossed the Potomac. As it turned out it was a false and dangerous assumption because Hooker had indeed moved northward paralleling Lee's movement. While all this was going on General Stuart, in one of his famous, cross-country dashes, had come within 10 miles of Washington D.C. He was wreaking havoc on Union supplies and had captured over 125 army supply wagons. But he did not report to Lee until the second day of the battle. Lee went into battle at Gettysburg without a clear understanding of the

Maj. Gen. James Ewell Brown (Jeb) Stuart CSA

James Ewell Brown (Jeb) Stuart was one of the most capable and flamboyant officers in the Confederate army. His reports on enemy positions and movements were highly accurate and Lee had relied heavily on them.

Acting under orders that were not explicit Stuart decided to make another one of his famous rides around the enemy lines while Lee was moving his three corps northward. Stuart made the ride and captured 125 wagons of Union materiels but had to use a lengthy route to move back to Lee's army, finally arriving on the second day of the battle.

Lee's patience was hard pressed but he ignored the plea of some of his officers to have Stuart court martialed. Stuart was killed at Yellow Tavern May 12, 1864. After his death, Lee said, "He never brought me a piece of false information."

11

placement of the Union army.

Stuart's failure to keep Lee informed of the whereabouts of the Union army was a major mistake, and he is the favorite whipping boy for the loss of the battle. Lee had other cavalry at his disposal, but he had become over dependent on Stuart's accurate information.

Both the Union and the Rebel armies were expecting a fight. Both wanted a favorable field from which to do battle. Lee had warned his three scattered corps leaders not to bring on a "general engagement" if they should come in contact with the enemy.

Both armies also surely wanted to consolidate their army. Lee had extended his forces by moving Ewell's corps some forty miles north of Gettysburg. Ewell was in fact very close to Harrisburg and ready to take the lightly guarded state capital.

On June 28, Lee, through Gen. Longstreet's spy, learned that the Union army was less than two day's march away, moving in his direction. He also learned that General Hooker had been replaced with General George Meade by President Lincoln who gladly accepted Hooker's resignation. This was not good news for Lee. He would rather have faced Hooker whom he had just recently trounced at Chancellorsville. Lee had considerable respect for Meade.

Lee then recalled General Ewell, who was itching to storm Harrisburg, ordering Ewell's divisions, led by Maj. Gens. Robert Rodes and Jubal Early, to concentrate near Chambersburg, about 25 miles northwest of Gettysburg. Later they were ordered directly to Gettysburg.

Both armies were now converging on Gettysburg, the Confederates from the north and west and the Union from the south. Overall Lee would get his army

Lt. Gen. Ambrose Powell (A.P.) Hill CSA

Ambrose Powell (A. P.) Hill was frequently described as impetuous, with a tendency to attack the enemy on inadequate information. This is what he did in his first corps command decision at Gettysburg. He sent Henry Heth's full division into Gettysburg to see what was there.

Heth was met with rapid fire from cavalry brigades under Union Gen. John Buford. Heth, also prone to engage in a fight, returned the fire and the battle of Gettysburg was underway. Hill's performance at Gettysburg was not noteworthy, and he should carry the blame for failure to give Lee a choice of battle sites. However, Hill had distinguished himself as one of the greatest Rebel division commanders and was the hero of Antietam, bringing his division into the fray just in time to save Jackson.

Hill fought throughout the war, possibly more than any other general, but he was frequently sick and unable to perform. He was killed one week before the war ended.

Maj. Gen. Henry Heth CSA

Henry Heth, was reported to be the only general in the rebel army whom Robert E. Lee called by his first name. He, like Lee, and five other division commanders, was a Virginian.

He shared the distinction with George Pickett of graduating last in his class at West Point. He was given a brigade in A. P. Hill's division under Jackson's Corps just in time to participate at Chancellorsville where he served well. Heth, prior to the war, took much interest in marksmanship and eventually the U. S. Army published his manual on rifles and how to use them. During the war the Union command republished Heth's manual deleting his by-line.

Heth must share the responsibility with A. P. Hill for the inadvertent start of the battle of Gettysburg, but most historians give Hill the larger share, while others claim Lee could have pulled Heth's division back even after the firing started.

14

in place about half a day ahead of his enemy's.

The impetuous leader of the Confederate Third Corps, Lt. Gen. A. P. Hill, another brand-new corps leader, would not believe his subordinates that regular Union troops were already in the town of Gettysburg. Hill was a feisty little fighter who handled his men well but was prone to shoot from the hip on occasion. Lee believed Hill was the best choice to head the Third Corps, also brand-new. Some sources accused Lee of favoritism in selecting Hill who was, like Lee, a Virginian. Five out of Lee's nine division commanders were Virginia natives. Some felt another Hill, D. H. Hill, from South Carolina, would have been a better choice.

A. P. Hill, apparently unconcerned about Lee's order to guard against a major engagement, decided to send troops into Gettysburg. He ordered two divisions led by Maj. Gens. W. Dorsey Pender and Henry Heth to move down the Chambersburg Pike towards the town. They were hoping to find some badly needed shoes for the corps.

Pender, though new to the job of division commander, had a good reputation as a fighter. At 29 he was one of the youngest major generals in either army. Ahead of Pender's division was Heth, another Virginian, in his first role as division leader. It is said that he was the only general Lee called by his first name. He distinguished himself at West Point by being the last academically in his class.

When Heth reached Gettysburg he did not find shoes. What he found was Brig. Gen. John Buford and his Union cavalry troops dismounted, firing breech-loading rifles in his direction. Heth returned fire and that was the start of the three day battle that was to cause more than 50,000 casualties and cost more than 7,000 lives.

Lee had not chosen the ground to fight on; it had been forced on him by over-zealous subordinates. Most students of the battle lay this mistake on A. P. Hill's shoulders. He allowed two untried division commanders to move into the vanguard of the Union army. It was certainly a military mistake to deny the supreme commander the opportunity to select the battlefield. By a stroke of fortune, however, Lee's troop disposition, at that moment, was potentially strong, with no thanks to anyone's design. And he could immediately field more men than the Union, which was rare. Hill's Corps was on hand and much of Ewell's and Longstreet's Corps were just a short march away. The only Union force on hand was Buford's cavalry division. Union Maj. Gen. John Reynolds's First Corps and Maj. Gen. Oliver Howard's XI Corps were on their way but it would be several hours before they reached the field. Lee, of course, at that time had only fragmentary information.

But the chance of destroying a significant piece of the Army of the Potomac was looming and more than Lee could resist and later when he had digested all the components of the situation he ordered a general offensive.

As the morning wore on the fighting increased. Maj. Gen. John Reynolds had just enough time to throw his troops into the battle before being killed by a Rebel sniper. His I Corps relieved the exhausted Buford cavalry. Then later the controversial XI Corps, defeated at Chancellorsville, came on the scene.

Gettysburg, from start to finish, was a battle of mistakes and they continued throughout the three-day struggle. Those errors and mishaps are still alive for today's military strategists and historians. At the same

A West Point Shootout?

UNION ARMY		age	West Point Graduate	Class rank
	Maj. Gen. George G. Meade	47	1835	19th
Corps				
I	Maj. Gen. John F. Reynolds	43	1841	26th
II	Maj. Gen. Winfield S. Hancock	39	1844	18th
III	Maj. Gen. Daniel E. Sickles	43	politician	
V	Maj. Gen. George Sykes	41	1842	39th
VI	Maj. Gen. John Sedgwick	49	1837	24th
XI	Maj. Gen. Oliver O. Howard	32	1854	4th
XII	Maj. Gen. Henry W. Slocum	35	1852	7th

CONFEDERATE ARMY				
	General Robert E. Lee	56	1829	2nd
1st Corps				
	Lt. Gen. James Longstreet	42	1842	54th
	Maj. Gen. Lafayette McLaws	42	1842	48th
	Maj. Gen. George E. Pickett	38	1846	last
	Maj. Gen. John B. Hood	34	1853	44th
2nd Corps				
	Lt. Gen. Richard Ewell	46	1840	13th
	Maj. Gen. Jubal A. Early	46	1837	18th
	Maj. Gen. Edward Johnson	47	1838	32nd
	Maj. Gen. Robert E. Rodes	34	1848 VMI	
3rd Corps				
	Lt. Gen. Ambrose P. Hill	37	1847	15th
	Maj. Gen. Richard H. Anderson	42	1842	40th
	Maj. Gen. Henry Heth	37	1847	last
	Maj. Gen. William D. Pender	29	1854	19th

time there was much gallant leadership and heroic action which is less well documented.

Some mistakes were of such a magnitude as to have turned the course of the battle. Others were a failure of leadership that in some cases caused the loss of hundreds of lives. Such mistakes collectively affected the momentum and disposition of fighting units and, no doubt, the shape of the final outcome.

With a few exceptions Gettysburg was a West Point competition between Academy graduates from the North and the South. Many fundamental military mistakes were made, some of them by non-professional soldiers, but the professionals made more than their share of the errors and most of the big ones. The shortage of well-trained field officers, particularly on the Confederate side, was apparent.

The Yankee and Rebel armies were organized quite differently. Rebel divisions were big, with up to 8000 men, almost as large as some Yankee corps. And rebel division generals had the same rank as Union corps generals – major general. Rebel corps leaders were given the exalted rank of Lt. General, offered very sparingly by the Union.

At Gettysburg the Union's seven corps numbered about 95,000 while the Confederacy's three corps numbered about 70,000 or about three to two which was a typical contest situation; in fact a better match-up than the Rebs usually enjoyed. The chart on page 17 shows the way the armies (infantry) were organized:

The average age of the Union corps commanders was 40.3 years, which compared almost identically to the Confederate division commander's 39.9. Academically, the Union generals fared slightly better due to the performance of Confederates George Pickett and Henry Heth who both finished last in

#4

Brig. Gen. Joseph Robert Davis CSA

Joseph Robert Davis, nephew of Confederate President Jefferson Davis was made a brigadier general apparently by way of nepotism. He certainly had no military training to recommend him.

He had the honor or misfortune, along with fellow brigadier James Archer, of launching the Battle of Gettysburg when the two brigades rode down the Chambersburg Pike and into a hornet's nest of Yankees. After a successful charge, Davis was ready to celebrate a victory, but he allowed his brigade to be trapped in a railroad cut where hundreds of his men were captured. Gen. Heth was later criticized for allowing the understrengthed, inexperienced brigade to lead the army.

But Davis' services were still in demand and his broken brigade was called on two days later to support Pickett's charge. He fought in all the major battles fo!lowing Gettysburg and stood in ranks April 9, 1865 when Lee surrendered at Appomatox.

#5

Brig. Gen. James J. Archer CSA

James J. Archer of Maryland was a competent general but too enthusiastic when he led the first wave of Heth's division down the Chambersburg Pike toward Gettysburg on the morning of July 1, 1863.

Archer's Brigade was on the right and the Confederate President's nephew, Robert Davis, was leading the brigade on the left. Suddenly Archer was surrounded by Union troops. An Alabama infantryman described the situation: "There were 20,000 Yanks down in among us hollering 'surrender!'" Archer's failure to reconnoiter caused his capture along with nearly all of his brigade.

He was the first Rebel general captured in Lee's army. After being dragged through Gettysburg to the jeers of onlookers, one of Archer's former associates, now a Union officer held out his hand and said, "Glad to see you General," to which Archer responded, "Well, I damn sure am not glad to see you." Archer was later exchanged but died Oct. 24, 1864.

their West Point class.

All of Meade's corps leaders were West Pointers with the exception of Dan Sickles, who fought his way up in rank to Major General by way of politics. Sickles, without permission, pulled his III Corps out of position on Cemetery Ridge on the second day exposing the flank of the Union line. He was severely criticized, but President Lincoln commended him for his aggressiveness.

All of Lee's division commanders were trained at the U. S. Military Academy except Robert Rodes, who had comparable training at Virginia Military Institute.

Tactical mistakes at Gettysburg started almost immediately after the first shot was fired on the western fringe of the little town that morning, Wednesday, July 1, 1863. Gen. Heth, the least experienced division commander in Lee's army, was first to strike. It was a poor start.

Heth's greenest brigadier, Joseph R. Davis, who apparently had no more military background to commend him than being the nephew of Confederate President Jefferson Davis, was detailed on a mission that got his regiments stuck in the deep cut of a railroad embankment and some 500 Rebels were taken prisoner. Almost at the same time, in an equally disastrous move, Brig. Gen. James J. Archer, another Heth brigade leader, was flanked by Union troops and ended up behind their lines and was captured – the first Rebel general in Lee's army ever captured. Hundreds of his men were killed, injured or captured. Heth was criticized for sending these two brigades, which were either under-strength or inexperienced, into the front of the battle.

Not long after that the Union XI Corps, which had been disgraced at Chancellorsville, arrived. One of its

Brig. Gen. Francis C. Barlow USA

Francis C. Barlow, at 28, was known as one of the "boy generals" and maybe the only clean-shaven Union general. He was a division commander at Gettysburg in the infamous XI Corps which had been beaten badly at Chancellorsville.

Inexplicably, on the first day of the battle, he moved his brigades away from a line held with the I Corp and jeopardized the already weakened effort to hold for more Union support. He was badly injured and left on the field where he was picked up later and cared for by Rebel Brig. Gen. John B. Gordon. Gordon thought Barlow had died and Barlow thought Gordon had been killed. They were introduced years later and learned what happened. They became close friends.

Barlow was a Harvard graduate and a strict disciplinarian. He was very unpopular with his corps largely composed of immigrants. Barlow claimed "The Dutch won't fight." He recovered from his injuries at Gettysburg and distinguished himself at Spotsylvania.

22

division leaders, clean-shaven, 29-year-old Brig. Gen. Francis Barlow, a Harvard graduate, quickly got the Corps in great trouble when he inexplicably moved off the battle line with I Corps. Later Barlow accused his immigrant troops of cowardice.

About noon Rebel Maj. Gen. Rodes arrived on the battle scene from the north in good position to attack the newly arrived Union XI Corps which had come to support the struggling I Corps.

Rodes ordered thrusts by the brigades of Brig. Gen. Alfred Iverson and Col. Edward A. O'Neal. Through failure to reconnoiter both these brigades were decimated while their leaders were well to the rear. Two more costly mistakes that slowed the Rebel advance.

The start of Day One at Gettysburg was disastrous for the Confederacy and revealed the army's shortages in field grade officers. The Union's officer problem seemed less severe.

Some of the blundering type mistakes were made by non-professional generals, although nearly always being poorly directed by senior ranked West Pointers.

Finally Hill puts Pender's Division into the fray. Early arrives from the northeast and the Confederates sweep the exhausted Union I and XI Corps, some in panic, back through the town of Gettysburg to the lofty protection of Cemetery Ridge. The Rebels win the field but it has cost them dearly in casualties, and their enemy is becoming well entrenched.

The Rebels have gained ground, but the Yankees are in better position than when the fighting started. They have the high ground. Rebel Gen. Ewell is then confronted with the question, never to be forgotten in the history of this battle, of whether he should attack Culp's Hill and Cemetery Hill - two commanding positions which could control the landscape for miles around, but were occupied by the Union. Ewell had orders from Lee to take the hills, if "practicable." Lee was used to giving discretion to his corps commanders. He always did so with "Stonewall" Jackson. But Ewell was not Jackson. He saw too many problems with the effort. In fact, it probably was not the easy task Ewell's critics made it seem to be years later. But in any event, a great tactical opportunity was lost.

Day Two at Gettysburg finds the Confederates occupying more ground than before including the town, but with each hour Union forces on Cemetery Ridge are becoming better fortified.

A mile south of Gettysburg, Rebel Generals Hood and McLaws, of Longstreet's Corps, suffer and inflict casualties by the thousands fighting in such places as Peach Orchard, Devil's Den, the Wheatfield, and Little Round Top. Union General Sickles's exposed flank is finally repaired by his disgusted colleagues. Brig. Gen. Ambrose W. Wright, a Georgian, breaks the Union line on Cemetery Ridge in a desperate charge, but Yankee reserves drive him off. Ewell finally attacks up Culp's Hill but he can't take it. Thousands die during the day.

On Day Three Ewell is pushed off of Culp's Hill. Lee again rejects Longstreet's plan to move around the Union left and perhaps develop a defensive position. The attack starts early in the afternoon with the greatest artillery battle in history. Lee hopes to soften the middle of the Union Army on Cemetery Ridge with the use of over 140 cannons. The Union answers in kind. General George Pickett with his three fresh brigades joined by eight others, moves out of the woods in Napoleonic lines stretching out about a mile. Of the 12,000 men who walk the open 1500 yards, scarcely one of two survives death, injury, or capture. Union cannons and muskets cut the men to

Lt. Gen. Richard S. Ewell CSA

Richard S. "Old Bald Head" Ewell, one of the favorite scapegoats for the loss at Gettysburg, was blamed for the failure of the Rebels to continue their victorious rout of Yankee forces on the first day of battle.

Hill's and Ewell's corps had pushed the Union I and XI corps back through the town of Gettysburg where they held a weak position on Culp's and Cemetery Hills. Lee ordered Ewell to take the hills if "practicable," but Ewell

declined. It was Ewell's first role as a corps commander and he was indecisive. Years later Union Gen. Winfield Hancock, who was present, said the Confederates would probably have been able to crush the disorganized Union corps.

To his credit Ewell had fought well with "Stonewall" Jackson and had pushed the Union out of Winchester, Va. shortly before the Gettysburg battle. The one-legged Ewell had to tie himself in the saddle.

Maj. Gen. Daniel Edgar Sickles USA

Daniel Edgar Sickles was one of the most controversial generals in the Union army. He was a politician and served in the U.S. Congress 1857-1861 from New York.

Meade's war plan on the second day was shattered when Sickles decided to move his III Corps off Cemetery Ridge where he held the left flank with the II Union Corp. Sickles thought the higher ground a thousand yards to the west would be a better choice. It turned out to be a near disaster. In the aggressive effort Sickles lost his leg. Before the war Sickles had gained notoriety when he shot and killed his wife's lover (the son of Francis Scott Key, author of the Star Spangled Banner). It was the first use of a "temporary insanity" plea in the courts.

After the war he blamed Meade for the unfortunate results of his ill-conceived advance, claiming Meade failed to take advantage of his move.

pieces. The charge fails. Lee heads for the Potomac. History's most destructive battle is over.

Whose mistake was it?

Lee said it was all his fault. Most historians are willing to believe him. But Lee was speaking tactically about the results of the fatal charge. The total military operation on both sides was littered with errors of judgment and tactics about which hundreds of books have been written.

Meade had won a battle, not a victory.

Lee's army was badly crippled but it was a fighting unit which continued to strike back for nearly two more years.

A clear victory could not be won by North or South by simply winning battles. As long as the South was able to wage war, there was no way for the North to win. The North had to crush the South's war machine. Meade, immediately after Gettysburg, had the opportunity to land what might have been a fatal blow to the South's fighting ability had he crushed Lee's ravaged forces before they crossed the Potomac - an opportunity he had for seven days. He had nearly double the number of effective soldiers. Most of his corps were still in fighting shape. The Union VI Corps, for instance, was virtually unscathed.

But Meade was a tactical thinker as most of his peers. He followed Lee to the Potomac River and waited for the perfect time to strike and it never came. The only participants of the Civil War who seemed to understand the North's need were its President, Abraham Lincoln, and a general named Grant. Meade let Lee sneak away in the dark.

Next to Lee's decision to fight it out at Gettysburg, Meade's failure to pursue him after the Confederate retreat was the greatest mistake of the battle.

But what about Lee? Did he have an alternative?

Lee was unsurpassed as a tactician. He has been most faulted for ordering the charge led by Pickett on the third day. The final charge turned out to be a terrible mistake, but most historians admit that Lee might have won on the final day had things worked as he planned. The Confederates might have broken the Union center. But things did not work as Lee planned. Ewell was unsuccessful on the enemy's right, Longstreet was sulky and late coming up, Confederate artillery fired too high, and plenty of other mistakes were made that weakened the total plan, including the loss of many of Lee's most capable officers and men on the first and second days.

In the end, Lee had overplayed his hand and must take the blame for the failure at Gettysburg, as he volunteered to do. The last real opportunity of the Confederacy had disappeared in the smoke between Seminary and Cemetery Ridges. The myth of Confederate invincibility had proven to be a false servant, a great mistake. Lee had depended on it.

Lee thought the South's demands could be met with one huge, glorious victory. He sought a negotiated peace. He knew total victory was impossible for the Confederacy. And indeed if Lee had prevailed at Gettysburg it might have changed our nation as we know it today, but probably not greatly. Neither North nor South was likely to give much ground on the issues of unionism or states rights, but perhaps, in the agony of the situation, some form of divine statesmanship could have brought the two sides to an accord.

Perhaps the South would have agreed to a plan that eliminated slavery with some small compensation to owners. The moral wrong of slavery had reached

#9

Gen. Robert E. Lee CSA

Gen. Robert E. Lee, Confederate commander at Gettysburg, hoped to crush the Union Army of the Potomac and perhaps seize Baltimore or Washington in order to force a negotiated peace.

A Rebel victory at Gettysburg would likely have defeated Lincoln's Republican party which supported the war. Lee could have entrenched in a defensive stand after routing Union forces on the battle's first day but he believed his best opportunity was to break the Union center. The final charge led by Pickett was disastrous but it might have succeeded had Lee's generals performed as planned.

Lee's army was badly disrupted after the victorious battle of Chancellorsville and he was left with untried corps commanders. His only veteran corps leader, James Longstreet, did not like Lee's plan and was sulky and sluggish in movement. Lee's greatest mistake may have been his belief that his troops were invincible.

29

#10

Maj. Gen. George G. Meade USA

George G. Meade took command of the Army of the Potomac just two days before the start of the Battle of Gettysburg. Lincoln was glad to get rid of Gen. "Fighting Joe" Hooker who had performed badly at Chancellorsville.

Lincoln's first choice was Gen. John Reynolds, but Reynolds made it clear he did not want the job, which Meade accepted reluctantly. Meade was a steady general who was cool under fire.

He liked to hold war councils with his generals to back up his own opinions. He held such a council July 2 asking his corps leaders whether they should attack Lee or remain entrenched. All his generals, and Meade himself, voted to stay on Cemetery Ridge.

Meade's great mistake was to fail to attack Lee while Lee worked seven days on the Potomac building a pontoon bridge for his troops to cross.

most owners and the economics of slavery were faltering. Maybe the North would have agreed to pay some reparations to the South and also reduce the burdensome tariff. The Union could have done all those things at much less cost than continuing the war.

It was perhaps too late in the war for Lee to employ the type of warfare the South needed to wear down the North. The North was desperately tired of sending men and money into the effort, but, and probably more rapidly, the South was shrinking in its ability to punish its opponent. Lee's string of victories had left huge casualties among his troops, many of whom could never be replaced.

Lee was aware of how strategy could aid the South, but skirting away from the fight went against his nature as a skilled offensive warrior. He knew the capture of Baltimore or Washington would be a coup to force the North to concede in some way. In fact such an accomplishment would make sense of the Pennsylvania campaign. But, as he told Longstreet, "The enemy is there and I am going to strike him."

Baltimore would have been the most logical target. It was larger, closer, and less protected. Its seizure would have given Lee leverage for negotiation.

After sweeping the I and XI Corps from the field in great disorder on the afternoon of the first day Lee, had he chosen to make a strategic move, might have marched after dark around the Union left as Longstreet had suggested earlier and moved rapidly to Baltimore via the Baltimore Pike. When Meade pursued, Lee could have taken a favorable defensive position at Pipe Creek, Meade's selection for a defensive position before arriving at Gettysburg. Supplies would have been a problem but Lee existed for seven days after the battle on the Potomac building a bridge. This move, as it turned out, would have had a much better chance of contributing to Southern strategy than two more days of slaughter at Gettysburg. But, remember, Stuart had not yet arrived; Lee did not know where Meade's army was. As it turned out only Sedgwick's VI Corps had failed to reach the Gettysburg area. Lee might have pulled it off. He was bold enough to try it, but he was at a great disadvantage without Jackson. Judging by the performance of his three corps commanders and the poor manner in which they coordinated, it is not difficult to understand Lee's probable apprehension.

The superb artilleryman at Gettysburg, Rebel General Edward Porter Alexander, believed to his death that Lee passed up a great opportunity at the end of the first day of battle. Alexander said Lee should have pulled forces to Seminary Ridge, dug in, and waited for Meade to attack. Psychologically, Lee had won the day, and Meade would have been forced to go on the offense. Alexander contended Seminary Ridge was not as good a position as Cemetery Ridge, but could have been defended easily.

That Gettysburg ever happened was the greatest mistake of all. But the enormity of the tragic conflict etched deeply the belief and truth that the nation must always remain one. In that way it provided a great service to us all.

Resources:
GETTYSBURG Battle & Battlefield by W.S. Storrick, reprinted by Barnes and Noble, 1993. THE GETTYS-BURG CAMPAIGN JUNE–JULY 1863 by Albert A. Nofi, Revised Edition, 1993. GETTYSBURG by Lt. Frank A. Haskell USA and Col. William C. Oates CSA, Edited by Paul Andrew Hutton, reprinted by Bantam Books, 1992. GETTYSBURG The Final Fury by Bruce Catton, Doubleday, 1974. THEY MET AT GETTYS-BURG by Edward J. Stackpole with prologue by Robert H. Fowler, Stackpole Books, Fourth Printing, 1986. THE FIRST DAY AT GETTYSBURG Essays on Confederate and Union Leadership edited by Gary W. Gallagher, Kent State University Press, 1992. LEE CONSIDERED by Alan T. Nolan, University of North Carolina Press, 1992. FIGHTING FOR THE CONFEDERACY Memoirs of Edward Porter Alexander, The University of North Carolina, 1993. STARS IN THEIR COURSES – The Gettysburg Campaign by Shelby Foote, 1994. THE CIVIL WAR Gettysburg High Tide, Time Life Books, 1987. GENERAL A.P. HILL The Story of a Confederate Warrior by James L. Robertson, Jr., Vintage Civil War Library, 1992. WHY THE SOUTH LOST THE CIVIL WAR by Richard E. Beringer, Herman Hattaway, Archer Jones, William N. Still, Jr., University of Georgia Press, 1986 . GETTYSBURG Culp's Hill and Cemetery Hill by Harry W. Planz, The University of North Carolina Press, 1993. JAMES LONGSTREET Lee's War Horse by H. J. Eckenrode and Bryan Conrad, The University of North Carolina Press, 1986.